LAST CHANCE TO SEE | ENDANGERED ANIMALS

ANITA GANERI

WAYLAND
www.waylandbooks.co.uk

LAST CHANCE TO SEE | ENDANGERED ANIMALS

First published in Great Britain in 2017
by Wayland

Editor: Sarah Silver
Designer: Alessandro Minoggi

ISBN: 978 1 5263 0189 5

MIX
Paper from
responsible sources
FSC® C104740
FSC
www.fsc.org

Printed and bound in China

Wayland, an imprint of
Hachette Children's Group
Part of Hodder and Stoughton
Carmelite House
50 Victoria Embankment
London EC4Y 0DZ

An Hachette UK Company
www.hachette.co.uk
www.hachettechildrens.co.uk

CONTENTS

ON THE EDGE

Scientists estimate that every year, tens of thousands of species of animals are becoming extinct or are in serious danger of dying out. Their habitats are being cleared to make more space for humans to live and farm in. They are being hunted and captured, often illegally, for meat, body parts, and for the pet trade. This is putting biodiversity seriously at risk.

UNHEALTHY BALANCE

Biodiversity means the amazing variety of plants and animals on planet Earth. It is the result of millions of years of evolution. A loss of biodiversity has a wide-reaching knock-on effect. In nature, living things are linked together. Different species rely on each other for their survival, and to maintain a balanced ecosystem. So if one species dies out, it affects many other plants and animals, too.

Coral reefs are one of the most diverse ecosystems on Earth, home to thousands of types of sea animals.

IMPORTANT INSECTS

Many species of bee are threatened with extinction because of the growing use of pesticides. Plants need bees or other animals to pollinate their flowers so that they can produce seeds and new plants. If the bees die out, so too will many plants, including those we rely on for our own food.

A conservationist working to reintroduce an orphaned western lowland gorilla back into the wild.

IUCN CLASSIFICATION

Animals at risk are given an IUCN classification. This is a rating set by the International Union for the Conservation of Nature (IUCN), based on the animal's risk of extinction. The most endangered species are placed on the IUCN's Red List, which helps to draw attention to them and to guide the actions of conservationists.

BACTRIAN CAMEL

(Camelus ferus)

Wild Bactrian camels live in the Gobi Desert, one of the harshest habitats on Earth. The desert is extremely dry, with temperatures ranging from -40ºC in winter to over 40ºC in summer. The camels travel vast distances across the desert, in search of food and water.

DESERT DESIGN

Bactrian camels are superbly adapted to desert life. Their hair is thick and shaggy in winter, but is shed in chunks during summer. They have double rows of long eyelashes to protect their eyes and can close their nostrils to keep out sand and dust. They can go for days without drinking, and can drink salty water if necessary. Their humps store fat for times when food is scarce.

STATS

LOCATION: China, Mongolia

NUMBERS IN THE WILD:
Fewer than 1,000

THREATENED BY: Hunting, habitat loss, competition with domestic camels and livestock

Domestic camels in the Gobi Desert, Mongolia.

FALLING NUMBERS

Today, there are fewer than 1,000 wild Bactrian camels left and their numbers are falling fast. They are found only in four remote locations in northwest China and southwest Mongolia. The largest group lives in China, in a stretch of desert that was used as a nuclear test site from 1955 till 1996. Astonishingly, the camels were not affected by the radiation.

HUNTED TO DEATH

For centuries, wild Bactrian camels have been hunted for their meat and skins. More recently, they have lost their habitat to mining and industry. This has pushed them into areas where they now compete for food and water with domestic camels and livestock. As a result, angry farmers will often hunt the wild camels.

URGENT ACTION

The governments of China and Mongolia, together with the Wild Camel Protection Foundation, are working to protect the camel and its fragile habitat. Two special reserves have been created – one in China; one in Mongolia. There are also plans to breed more camels in captivity, which could then be introduced back into the wild.

BLACK RHINOCEROS
(Diceros bicornis)

The black rhino lives in grasslands and forests in eastern and southern Africa. For many years, they have been killed for their meat and hide, and hunted for sport. Now, the greatest threat to their survival is the growing demand for rhino horn.

RHINO HABITS

The black rhino eats leaves and twigs, which it grasps with its flexible lips. Rhinos have sharp senses of smell and hearing, but very poor eyesight. If threatened, they can sprint surprisingly fast, at speeds of over 50 km/h. Despite its name, the black rhino is actually grey.

STATS

LOCATION: EASTERN AND SOUTHERN AFRICA

NUMBERS IN THE WILD: AROUND 3,600

THREATENED BY: HUNTING FOR SPORT, POACHING FOR HORN

MEDICINAL HORN

Rhino horn is worth a huge amount of money, and today, almost all rhino deaths are caused by poachers. The main market for horn is parts of Asia, where it is used in a traditional type of medicine that is thousands of years old. The horn is ground up into a powder and mixed with hot water. It is believed to cure illnesses, such as fever and rheumatism.

Rhino horn is also used to make very precious dagger handles.

RHINOS AT RISK

Black rhinos once roamed all over Africa, south of the Sahara Desert, but today, they are extremely rare. Between 1970-1992, it is estimated that numbers crashed from around 65,000 to 2,300. They have now recovered to around 3,600 but the rhino is still in grave danger from poachers.

A rhino having its horn removed by conservationists to protect it from poachers.

URGENT ACTION

Despite being illegal, trade in rhino horn still continues, so many wild rhinos now live in heavily protected reserves, patrolled by armed anti-poaching teams. On some reserves, the rhinos have had their horns painlessly removed by vets to try to put the poachers off. There are also plans to develop artificial rhino horn that could be used in Asian medicine.

9

CHINESE GIANT SALAMANDER

(Andrias davidianus)

The Chinese giant salamander is the world's largest amphibian, reaching up to 1.8 m in length and weighing up to 50 kg. It lives in cold, fast-flowing mountain streams in China, and has many adaptations for its lifestyle. Unlike fish, it does not have gills for breathing, but absorbs oxygen through its wrinkled skin.

STATS

LOCATION: China

NUMBERS IN THE WILD:
NOT KNOWN

THREATENED BY:
HABITAT LOSS, HARVESTING FOR FOOD

LOSING HABITAT

Over the last 30 years, the number of Chinese giant salamanders in the wild has fallen dramatically, and today, they are very rare. One reason for this is the destruction of their stream habitat. The building of dams has changed the way the streams flow, and some have dried up completely. The water has also been polluted by farming and mining activities.

10

A DELICACY

Salamander meat is considered a delicacy in China. Some salamanders are raised on farms but most of those killed for food come from the wild. These salamanders are easy to hook out of their hiding holes in the stream bank, and hunters also use dynamite, electric shocks and pesticides to kill them.

The Mount Wuyi nature reserve in southeast China.

SALAMANDER FARMING

A growing problem is the number of captive salamanders that are released from farms. They can spread diseases to wild salamanders. One solution is to make sure that captive and wild salamanders are kept strictly apart. Conservationists are suggesting tagging captive salamanders with microchips so that they are easy to identify. New stock should also be quarantined to make sure that it is healthy.

URGENT ACTION

Conservationists are also looking at ways of protecting the salamanders' stream habitat. Since the 1980s, many salamander reserves have been set up in China. They include Mount Wuyi nature reserve. There are fears, however, that plans to bring more tourists into this reserve are making it difficult to keep the salamanders' habitat pollution-free and healthy.

DEVIL'S HOLE PUPFISH
(Cyprinodon diabolis)

Growing to a length of just 25 mm, the tiny Devil's Hole pupfish may be the rarest fish in the world. It is found in only one place – a deep pool, known as 'Devil's Hole', in the middle of the scorching Mojave Desert in the USA. The pool is no bigger than an average room in a house, but it is where every member of this species has ever lived.

ON THE SHELF

The pupfish's isolated pool lies in a limestone cavern, which is open to the air. It is fed with water from an aquifer and stays at a constant, warm temperature of around 33°C. The pool starts 15 m below the surface of the ground, and is thought to be over 200 m deep. At one end, there is a limestone shelf where the pupfish gather to feed on algae and breed.

The Devil's Hole pool.

STATS

LOCATION: USA

NUMBERS IN THE WILD: AROUND 115

THREATENED BY: WATER LOSS, EARTHQUAKES, FLASH FLOODS

ON THE BRINK

With such a small habitat, the number of Devil's Hole pupfish has never been very high. Over the last 40 years, though, it has dropped sharply, and there may only be around 115 fish left. As people pump out groundwater for drinking and farming, the water level in Devil's Hole is dropping, putting the fish at serious risk.

A spring in the Ash Meadows National Wildlife Refuge.

PUPFISH PROTECTION

In 1984, the Ash Meadows National Wildlife Refuge was set up to protect Devil's Hole and the surrounding area of desert. The Refuge is home to many other species of plants and animals that are found nowhere else on Earth. Scientists monitor the water level in the Devil's Hole pool every day and have begun to feed the fish a special food to increase their numbers.

URGENT ACTION

Scientists have been trying to set up 'refuge populations' of the pupfish. This means breeding the fish in captivity in case they are wiped out in the wild. So far, these efforts have not been successful but there are plans to build new types of tank that copy water and food conditions in Devil's Hole more closely. This way, the fish feel more at home.

GIANT IBIS

(*Thaumatibis gigantea*)

A huge bird, the giant ibis is found mainly in northern Cambodia, with a small population in southern Laos. It lives around forest swamps, marshes and rivers. The ibis looks striking, with a bald head and neck, a long bill that curves downwards, and dark red eyes. It can also be recognised by its loud, ringing call.

FEEDING TIME

The ibis is well adapted to its habitat, using its long beak to probe the mud or water for food. It mainly eats insects, such as cicadas and locusts, together with eels, frogs and shellfish. The ibis often feeds in the soft mud around watering holes, dug by water buffalo and other large animals.

IBIS IN DANGER

Giant ibis were once found all over southeast Asia, but today, they are extinct in Vietnam and Thailand, and very rare in other parts of their range. Experts estimate that there may be fewer than 230 pairs left. They are hunted by people for their meat and eggs, which are also eaten by animal predators, such as martens and civets.

LOCATION: Cambodia, Laos

NUMBERS IN THE WILD: Fewer than 230 pairs

THREATENED BY: Habitat loss, hunting, human activities

Vital ibis habitats are being lost due to rubber plantations like this one in Cambodia.

HABITAT LOSS

The ibis is also losing its habitat, and its feeding and breeding sites. Forests are being cut down to clear space for rubber and teak plantations, and wetlands are being cleared for farmland. In the dry season, humans are also taking over the birds' watering holes, forcing the birds to wander further and further to find food and drink.

URGENT ACTION

Various steps are being taken by conservationists to try to protect the giant ibis, especially its nesting sites high up in the forest trees. Scientists have been locating ibis nests and fitting smooth, plastic belts to the base of the trees. This stops predators from being able to climb up the trees to reach the ibis eggs. But this project alone is not enough to save this very rare bird from extinction.

HAIRY-NOSED WOMBAT
(Lasiorhinus krefftii)

The northern hairy-nosed wombat lives in grasslands and eucalyptus woodlands in Australia. Built for digging, it has short, powerful legs and strong claws. It digs burrows for sleeping and breeding, and can dig a new burrow in a day. Like a kangaroo, the female has a pouch, but the wombat's pouch opens backwards so that it does not fill with earth as it digs.

UNDER THREAT

Threats to the northern hairy-nosed wombat include losing its habitat to farmland and being eaten by predators, such as dingoes. The wombats are also in danger from natural events, such as wildfires, floods and droughts. Today, there are only around 200 northern hairy-nosed wombats left in the wild, making it the rarest of Australia's marsupials.

SOLE SURVIVORS

Most of the surviving wombats live in one single colony in Epping Forest National Park, Queensland. They are protected by a 2-m-high fence, aimed at keeping dingoes and other predators out. The fence was built in 2002, after a pack of dingoes killed at least 10 wombats.

An aerial view of Epping Forest National Park.

WOMBAT MONITORING

To further protect the wombats, Epping Forest National Park is not open to the public, only to rangers and scientists. The scientists use remote cameras to photograph the wombats when they come out of their burrows to feed at night. They also collect samples of wombat hair on sticky tape stretched across burrow entrances. Using DNA from the hair, the scientists can identify individual wombats and see how many there are.

Scientists sometimes trap the wombats to tag them.

STATS

LOCATION: Australia

NUMBERS IN THE WILD: Around 200

THREATENED BY: Habitat loss, predators

URGENT ACTION

There is a real danger that a single wildfire or flood could wipe out all the Epping Forest wombats. To lessen the risk, scientists are trying to establish other groups in different places. A second group has now been set up in Richard Underwood Nature Refuge, also in Queensland. It is made up of nine wombats taken from Epping Forest.

KAKAPO
(Strigops habroptila)

The kakapo from New Zealand is a large parrot that lives in forests and grasslands. It has wings, but cannot fly. Instead, it uses its large, strong legs for running and can also climb trees, using its powerful beak and claws. Unlike most parrots, the kakapo is nocturnal. During the day, it roosts in trees or on the ground, then comes out at night to look for food.

UNDER ATTACK

When a kakapo is under threat, it freezes completely still until the danger passes. Unfortunately, this behaviour, combined with its strong, musty smell, makes it an easy target. In the past, kakapo were hunted by the Maori people and their dogs. Now they are preyed on by cats, rats and stoats. Huge areas of their habitat have also been cleared for farming.

STATS

LOCATION: New Zealand

NUMBERS IN THE WILD:
Around 125

THREATENED BY:
Hunting, predators, habitat loss

ISLAND LIFE

Kakapo once lived all over New Zealand. Today, they are extinct across most of their range and the surviving kakapo have been moved from the mainland to three specially managed small islands – Codfish and Anchor Islands, off the South Island, and Little Barrier Island, off the North Island.

KAKAPO RECOVERY

A team of conservationists from Kakapo Recovery in New Zealand work tirelessly to protect and manage the kakapo population. Four members of the team live on Codfish and Anchor Islands, making sure that the birds are safe, well-fed and healthy. To keep tabs on the birds, the team fit them with transmitters that send out radio signals to report their location, whether they are nesting, and other information.

URGENT ACTION

Plans are now in place to find two further islands where the birds can live and breed in safety. The islands will first have to be cleared of rats and stoats before the kakapo can move in. Eventually, scientists hope to be able to reintroduce kakapos to the mainland, but this will take a lot more work.

LEATHERBACK TURTLE
(Dermochelys coriacea)

The leatherback turtle is the largest turtle, and one of the biggest reptiles in the world. Its body is designed for life at sea, with powerful flippers for swimming. These turtles swim vast distances across the oceans between their nesting and feeding sites, searching for jellyfish to eat.

NESTING BEACHES

The turtles spend most of their time at sea, but females come ashore to breed. They dig holes in the soft sand with their flippers, and lay around 110 eggs in the nest. After about 60 days, the eggs hatch. The baby turtles dig their way out and begin their hazardous journey to the sea. Many are eaten by crabs and seabirds before they reach the water.

Newly hatched baby leatherback turtles ready to make their way to the sea.

IN DECLINE

Over the last 20 years, numbers of leatherback turtles have fallen dramatically. Thousands are accidentally caught in fishing nets and drown because they cannot reach the surface to breathe. Thousands more are killed by eating plastic bags dumped into the sea. In some places, the turtles' nesting beaches are also being destroyed by the building of tourists resorts.

Turtles can mistake plastic bags for jellyfish.

These turtle eggs are being collected as part of a conservation programme.

POACHED EGGS

In many countries, collecting turtle eggs is illegal, but it is still a serious problem on some turtle nesting beaches. In southeast Asia, tens of thousands of eggs are taken for food each year. This has led to leatherback turtles becoming extinct in Malaysia. Adult turtles are also caught for their meat and shells.

STATS

LOCATION: PACIFIC, ATLANTIC, INDIAN OCEANS

NUMBERS IN THE WILD: 20,000 TO 30,000 NESTING FEMALES

THREATENED BY: FISHING NETS, DIGESTING PLASTIC, THEFT OF EGGS, HABITAT LOSS

URGENT ACTION

Conservation groups, such as the Leatherback Trust, are working with local people to save the turtles' habitat. Many nesting beaches have been set aside as sanctuaries. Teams of local rangers patrol the beaches and protect the nests from poachers. Eco-tourism is also being encouraged, so that tourists can visit the beaches and see the turtles, without doing them any harm.

MOUNTAIN CHICKEN

(Leptodactylus fallax)

The mountain chicken is a frog that once lived on seven Caribbean islands, but is now only found on two: Dominica and Montserrat. Hunted for their meat, which is said to taste like chicken, mountain chickens have been pushed to the brink of extinction.

SUPER FROGS

Adult mountain chickens can grow up to 22 cm long, making them one of the world's biggest frogs. They have large bodies and heads, and powerful back legs. They are usually found near springs and streams, where they lie in wait for prey, such as insects, millipedes, small frogs and even snakes.

The Caribbean island Montserrat is thought to have only one pair of mountain chickens remaining.

LOCATION: Dominica, Montserrat

NUMBERS IN THE WILD: Around 100

THREATENED BY: Disease, hunting, natural disasters

Captive breeding programmes like this one in Jersey, UK, are helping to increase the frog's population.

FROG FOOD

For years, mountain chickens were hunted for their meat, with tens of thousands of frogs being killed every year. Their large size and loud call made them an easy target. Hunting is now banned, but numbers have plummeted. One problem is that mountain chickens only have small broods of tadpoles, which means that it takes longer for their numbers to recover.

FATAL FUNGUS

An even bigger threat now faces the mountain chicken. In the 2000s, a deadly disease, caused by a fungus, struck their habitats, wiping out a staggering 99 per cent of the frogs. The fungus attacks their skin, through which they breathe, leading to cardiac arrest.

URGENT ACTION

After the outbreak of the fungus, 50 healthy mountain chickens were airlifted off the islands and sent to zoos around the world. Special nest burrows were built from modelling clay to mimic conditions in the wild. Since then, dozens have been released back into the wild, in places that are fungus-free. But there's a long way to go before the frog isn't on the IUCN's Red List.

TIGER
(Panthera tigris)

One of the largest big cats, tigers live in forests and mangrove swamps where they stalk their prey of deer and wild pigs. Each tiger has its own territory, and is solitary, meaning it usually hunts and lives on its own.

SHRINKING RANGE

Tigers once lived right across Asia, from Turkey to eastern Russia. Today, they are scattered across 13 countries. Some kinds of tigers, such as the Bali, Caspian and Javan tigers, are already extinct. The rest are all under threat from habitat loss and hunting. Despite laws banning the trade in tiger body parts, many are still being killed for their bones, which are used in Asian medicine.

STATS

LOCATION: ASIA

NUMBERS IN THE WILD: AROUND 3,890

THREATENED BY: HUNTING, HABITAT LOSS, CONFLICT WITH HUMANS

TIGER NUMBERS

From 100,000 at the beginning of the 20th century, tiger numbers had dropped to 3,200 a hundred years later. Today, numbers have risen to around 3,890, thanks to years of work by conservation groups, such as the World Wildlife Fund (WWF). In 2010, the 13 countries where tigers are found joined WWF in a project, called TX2, which aims to double tiger numbers by 2022.

Conservation areas can provide a safe habitat for tigers.

TIGER VERSUS HUMANS

It can be difficult for humans and tigers to live side-by-side. As the forests shrink and their prey becomes harder to find, tigers are being forced to hunt cattle and other livestock, which local people rely on for their livelihood. This leads to conflict with farmers, and tigers are often poisoned and killed, then sold for their skin and bones.

Tiger skins in China.

URGENT ACTION

In 1973, the Indian government set up Project Tiger to protect the country's remaining tigers. A Tiger Protection Force works to catch poachers and to keep the tigers safe. The project is also working with villagers whose lands lie next to the reserves, to reduce the risk of tiger attacks on humans. But much more work is needed to protect this vunerable species that has lost 93 per cent of its original habitat range.

WESTERN LOWLAND GORILLA
(Gorilla gorilla gorilla)

Western lowland gorillas can stand as tall as an adult human and can weigh 140 kg. They live in groups of up to 20 gorillas, led by an older male, with several females and their young. Over the last 25 years, the gorillas' numbers have declined by more than 60 per cent because of poaching, habitat loss and disease.

FOREST HOME

Spread across west Africa, the western lowland gorilla lives in lowland tropical rainforests and near swamps. It spends most of its time on the ground, but will climb trees to reach fruit – its main food – and build nests for sleeping in at night. Every day, western lowland gorillas may roam up to 4 km in search of the best fruit trees.

KILLED FOR MEAT

The gorillas' forest habitat is being cleared at an alarming rate for timber and to make space for farmland. This makes it easier for illegal hunters to find and kill gorillas for their meat. This 'bushmeat' is eaten by local people and demand is growing.

 STATS

LOCATION: West Africa

NUMBERS IN THE WILD: Unknown

THREATENED BY:
Hunting, habitat loss, disease

DEADLY DISEASE

Western lowland gorillas are also under serious threat from disease, especially the deadly Ebola virus. Some scientists estimate that Ebola has killed around a third of the entire population of wild gorillas, mostly western lowland gorillas. In some places, the figure is closer to 90 per cent. This is also putting humans at risk, because Ebola can be spread through handling and eating bushmeat.

This sign in the Congo warns visitors that the area is infected with Ebola.

ATTENTION EBOLA!
NE TOUCHONS JAMAIS,
NE MANIPULONS JAMAIS
LES ANIMAUX TROUVÉS
MORTS EN FORÊT

URGENT ACTION

Because gorilla meat is an important source of food and income for many local people, organisations, such as the Zoological Society of London (ZSL) are working to find alternatives. The ZSL project is looking at helping local people to grow more crops and raise more fish and livestock, rather than hunting gorillas and chimpanzees.

VAQUITA
(Phocoena sinus)

The vaquita is a porpoise that is only found in the northern end of the Gulf of California, Mexico. It lives in shallow lagoons along the shore where the water can reach 30ºC. It is the only type of porpoise to live in such warm water. Unfortunately, the number of vaquita has fallen so rapidly that it is the most endangered cetacean in the world.

VAQUITA FEATURES

The vaquita has a stocky, dark-grey body, with a white underside and large black rings around its mouth and eyes. It is difficult to see in the wild because it comes to the surface slowly to breathe, then quickly disappears again. It feeds mainly on fish and squid, found near the bottom of the sea.

LOCATION: Mexico

NUMBERS IN THE WILD: Around 60

THREATENED BY: Unintenional capture in illegal fishing nets

FACING EXTINCTION

By 2014, the number of vaquita had fallen below 100, putting it in serious danger of becoming extinct. Since then, the situation has got even worse and there are now only about 60 vaquita left. If urgent action is not taken, scientists estimate that the vaquita could die out before 2025 – time is running out fast.

DEADLY CATCH

The most serious threat to the vaquita's survival is being accidentally entangled in fishing nets, which are set to catch fish and sharks. The vaquita cannot get to the surface to breathe and so they drown. Young vaquita are most likely to be caught. In most of the vaquita's habitat, fishing is officially banned, but still continues illegally.

A vaquita caught alongside other sea life in a fishing net.

Fishing in the Gulf of California, Mexico.

URGENT ACTION

The Mexican government is working with conservationists to bring the vaquita back from the brink. The most important measure is to ban the use of fishing nets, but this has a serious effect on local people who depend on fishing for their living. More work is needed to find alternative sources of income and to develop alternative types of fishing gear that will not harm the vaquita.

GLOSSARY

AMPHIBIAN
An animal, such as a frog, toad or salamander, which spends part of its life in water and part on land.

AQUIFER
A section of underground rock that can contain or carry water.

BIODIVERSITY
The variety of plants and animals in the world or in a particular habitat.

BROODS
Groups of bird or amphibian eggs laid together.

BUSHMEAT
The meat of African wild animals that is used as food.

CARDIAC ARREST
When a heart stops beating.

CETACEAN
A sea mammal, such as a whale, dolphin or porpoise.

CONSERVATIONIST
A person who works to protect the natural world and its wildlife.

DOMESTIC (ANIMAL)
An animal that is tame and kept by humans, often on a farm.

ECOSYSTEM
A place and the plants and animals that live in it, and depend on each other.

EUCALYPTUS
A fast-growing, evergreen tree originally from Australia. It has a strong-smelling oil in its leaves.

EXTINCT
When an animal or plant has died out, and no longer exists.

FUNGUS
A living thing, with no leaves or roots, such as mould and mushrooms.

GILLS
Parts of fish and some amphibians that are used for breathing.

GROUNDWATER
Water that is held underground in the soil or in cracks in rocks.

LAGOON
A stretch of seawater separated from the sea by a sandbank or coral reef.

LIVESTOCK
Farm animals, such as cattle and sheep.

MARSUPIAL
A type of mammal that is not completely developed when born and is carried around in a pouch.

OXYGEN
A gas that is in air and water and is necessary for people, animals and plants to live.

PESTICIDE
A chemical used for killing pests, especially insects.

PLANTATIONS
Huge farms on which crops, such as coffee, sugar and bananas are grown.

POACHER
A person who hunts and catches animals illegally (against the law).

POLLUTED
When the environment has been damaged, for example by chemicals or litter.

QUARANTINED
To keep an animal on its own for a while to make sure that it does not pass on any illnesses or diseases.

REFUGE POPULATION
A group of endangered animals kept in a safe place to make sure that they do not die out.

RHEUMATISM
A disease that makes the muscles and joints stiff, swollen and painful.

SPECIES
A set of plants or animals which have the same main characteristics and are able to breed with each other.

WETLANDS
Land made up of swamps and marshes.